The Heart of a Woman and Other Poems

The Heart of a Woman and Other Poems

Georgia Douglas Johnson

MINT EDITIONS

The Heart of a Woman and Other Poems was first published in 1918.

This edition published by Mint Editions 2021.

ISBN 9781513290683 | E-ISBN 9781513293530

Published by Mint Editions®

MINT EDITIONS

minteditionbooks.com

Publishing Director: Jennifer Newens
Design & Production: Rachel Lopez Metzger
Project Manager: Micaela Clark
Typesetting: Westchester Publishing Services

Contents

INTRODUCTION

The poems in this book are intensely feminine and for me this means more than an thing else that they are deeply human. We are yet scarcely aware, in spite of our boasted twentieth-century progress, of what lies deeply hidden, of mystery and passion, of domestic love and joy and sorrow, of romantic visions and practical ambitions, in the heart of a woman. The emancipation of woman is yet to be wholly accomplished; though woman has stamped her image on every age of the world's history, and in the heart of almost every man since time began, it is only a little over half of a century since she has either spoke or acted with a sense of freedom. During this time she has made little more than a start to catch up with man in the wonderful things he has to his credit; and yet all that man has to his credit would scarcely have been achieved except for the devotion and love and inspiring comradeship of woman.

Here, then, is lifted the veil, in these poignant songs and lyrics. To look upon what is revealed is to give one a sense of infinite sympathy; to make one kneel in spirit to the marvelous patience, the wonderful endurance, the persistent faith, which are hidden in this nature.

> *The heart of a woman falls back with the night.*
> *And enters some alien cage in its plight,*
> *And tries to forget it has dreamed of the stars*
> *While it breaks, breaks, breaks on the sheltering bars*
> *sings the poet. And the songs of the singer*
> *Are tones that repeat the cry of the heart*
> *Till it ceases to beat.*

This verse just quoted is from "The Dreams of the Dreamer," and with the previous quotation tells us that this woman's heart is keyed in the plaintive, knows the sorrowful agents of life and experience which knock and enter at the door of dreams. But women have made the saddest songs of the world, Sappho no less than Elizabeth Barrett Browning, Ruth the Moabite poetess gleaning in the fields of Boaz no less than Amy Levy, the Jewess who broke her heart against the London pavements; and no less does sadness echo its tender and appealing sigh in these songs and lyrics of Georgia Douglas Johnson.

But sadness is a kind of felicity with woman,
paradoxical as it may seem; and it is so be—
cause through this inexplicable felicity they
touched, intuitionally caress, reality.

So here engaging life at its most reserved sources, whether the form or substance through which it articulates be nature, or the seasons, touch of hands or lips, love, desire, or any of the emotional abstractions which sweep like fire or wind or cooling water through the blood, Mrs. Johnson creates just that reality of woman's heart and experience with astonishing raptures. It is a kind of privilege to know so much about the secrets of woman's nature, a privilege all the more to be cherished when given, as in these poems, with such exquisite utterance, with such a lyric sensibility.

William Stanley Braithwaite

THE HEART OF A WOMAN

The heart of a woman goes forth with the dawn,
As a lone bird, soft winging, so restlessly on,
Afar o'er life's turrets and vales does it roam
In the wake of those echoes the heart calls home.

The heart of a woman falls back with the night,
And enters some alien cage in its plight,
And tries to forget it has dreamed of the stars
While it breaks, breaks, breaks on the sheltering bars.

The Dreams of the Dreamer

The dreams of the dreamer
    Are life-drops that pass
The break in the heart
    To the souls hour-glass.

The songs of the singer
    Are tones that repeat
The cry of the heart
    'Till it ceases to beat.

GOSSAMER

The peerless boon of innocence,
    The first in nature's list,
Is fading, ere the rising sun
    The world awake has kist.

The early dew upon the grass,
    The purity of morn,
The glint that lies in virgin cheek.
    Frail cobwebs—of the dawn.

Sympathy

My joy leaps with your ecstasy,
  In sympathy divine;
The smiles that wreathe upon your lips.
  Find sentinels on mine:

Your lightest sigh I'm echoing,
  I tremble with your pain,
And all your tears are falling
  In my heart like bitter rain.

Contemplation

We stand mute!
No words can paint such fragile imagery,
Those prismic gossamers that roll
Beyond the sky-line of the soul;
We stand mute!

DEAD LEAVES

The breaking dead leaves 'neath my feet
A plaintive melody repeat,
Recalling shattered hopes that lie
As relics of a bygone sky.

Again I thread the mazy past,
Back where the mounds are scattered fast—
Oh! foolish tears, why do you start,
To break of dead leaves in the heart?

Dawn

Trailing night's sand-sifted stars,
Rainbows sweep, as day unbars.
Fragrant essences of morn,
Bathe humanity—new-born!

ELEVATION

There are highways in the soul,
    Heights like pyramids that rise
    Far beyond earth-veiled eyes,
    Sweeping through the barless skies
    O'er the line where daylight dies—
There are highways in the soul!

PEACE

I rest me deep within the wood,
　　Drawn by its silent call,
Far from the throbbing crowd of men
　　On nature's breast I fall.

My couch is sweet with blossoms fair,
　　A bed of fragrant dreams,
And soft upon my ear there falls
　　The lullaby of streams.

The tumult of my heart is stilled,
　　Within this sheltered spot.
Deep in the bosom of the wood.
　　Forgetting, and—forgot!

WHITHER?

Minutes swiftly throb and pass,
    Shadows cross the dial-glass,
Speeding ever to some call,
    Weary world and shadows, all.

Down the closing aisles of day,
    Tramping footsteps die away,
But no tidings thread the gloom,
    From the hushed and silent tomb.

QUEST

The phantom happiness I sought
    O'er every crag and moor;
I paused at every postern gate,
    And knocked at every door;

In vain I searched the land and sea,
    E'en to the inmost core,
The curtains of eternal night
    Descend—my search is o'er.

MATE

Our separate winding ways we trod,
Along the highways, unto God,
Unbonded by the clasp of hand,
Without a vow—we understand.
Estranged for aye, the fusing kiss.
Omnipotent, we bide in this—
They need no trammeling of bars
Whose souls were welded with the stars.

Emblems

A wordless kiss, a stifled sigh,
A trembling lip, a downcast eye,
   Alas, "they say,
   A-day, a-day,"
The cruse has failed, the lamp must die!

Mirrored

When lone and solitaire within your chamber,
  With lamp unlit, as evening shades unroll.
If you reveal the trail your thoughts are taking,
  I then may read the riddle of your soul.

For it is then, the tired mind unveiling,
  Drifts stark into the holy after-glow.
Within the hour of quiet meditation.
  The tidal thoughts, like limpid waters, flow.

Repulse

Nobody cares when I am glad,
    I beat upon their hearts in glee,
    "Drink, drink joy's brimming cup with me,"
    All echoless, my ecstasy—
Nobody cares when I am glad.

Nobody cares when I am sad,
    Whene'er I seek compassion's breast,
    I falter wounded from my quest
    Back! back into my heart, sore prest—
Nobody cares when I am sad.

QUERY

Is she the sage who will not sip
The cup love presses to her lip?
Or she who drinks the mad cup dry,
And turns with smiling face—to die?

PENT

The rain is falling steadily
    Upon the thirsty earth,
While dry-eyed, I remain, and calm
    Amid my own heart's dearth.

Break! break!! ye flood-gates of my tears
    All pent in agony,
Rain, rain! upon my scorching soul
    And flood it as the sea!!

Pages from Life

Not for your tender eyes that shine,
Nor for your red lips pulsing wine,
I love you, dear: your soul divine.
In sweet captivity, holds mine!

The tender eyes have lost their glow,
The flagons of the lips run low.
The autumn trembles in the air,—
A woman passes solitaire!

RECALL

Winter—aback sweeps the inward eye,
Fleet o'er the trail to a rose-wreathed sky,
Girt by a cordon of dreams I dwell
Deep in the heart of the old-time spell.

Almost, the tones of your whispered word,
Almost! the thrill that your dear lips stirred,
Almost!! that wild pulsing throb again—
Almost!!!—

         ('Tis winter, the falling rain).

GETHSEMANE

Into the garden of sorrow,
Some day we all must roam,
If not today, then tomorrow,
Bow 'neath its purple dome.
Out from the musk-laden banqueting halls,
Doffing our mirth-spangled vestments like thralls,
Softly we wend to Gethsemane,
In the hour that sorrow calls!

IMPELLED

Athwart the sky the great sun sails,
Through seons thus, the daylight trails,
And man, living breath of the sod
Beholding, in his heart knows God.

Throughout the night's long brooding deep,
Earth's trustful children die-to-sleep.
But with the whisperings of morn
Awake, unto the day, new-born.

The mystery of earth untold,
The great infinite, none behold,
Forge ever new the spiral chain,
Revolving man to God again.

EVENTIDE

The silence of the brooding night,
Enfolds me with its eerie light;
I lie upon its shadowed breast
A pilgrim, wearying for rest

Nightfall! thy sable curtains steep
My very soul in solace deep,
God sends thee with thy soothing balms,
That I may falter to thy arms.

THRALL

Fragile, tiny, just a sprite,
Holding me a thrall bedight,
Stronger than a giant's wand
Serves the word of your command.

Out from rushing worlds, though low
Should you whisper, I would know,
And would answer, though the breath
Be the gateway unto death.

YOUTH

The dew is on the grasses, dear,
    The blush is on the rose.
And swift across our dial-youth,
    A shifting shadow goes.

The primrose moments, lush with bliss,
    Exhale and fade away,
Life may renew the Autumn time,
    But nevermore the May!

JOY

There's a soft rosy glow o'er the whole world today,
There's a freshness and fragrance that trembles in May,
There's a lilt in the music that vibrates and thrills
From the uttermost glades to the tops of the hills.

Oh! I am so happy, my heart is so light.
The shades and the shadows have vanished from sight,
This wild pulsing gladness throbs like a sweet pain—
O soul of me, drink, ere night falleth again!

POSTHUMOUS

Of what avail the tardy showers,
To the famished summer flowers?
All in vain the rain-drops cry,
Dead things never make reply.

Life's belated cup of bliss,
Woo the weary lips to kiss,
When the singing is a sigh.
Pulses quivering, to die.

Omega

The fragile fabric of our dream
Drifts as a feather down life's stream
The long defile of empty days
Grim silhouetted, mock my gaze.

Though oft escapes the stifled sigh,
A desert ever broods my eye—
Since you have utterly forgot,
God grant that I remember not!

Tears and Kisses

There are tears sweet, refreshing like dewdrops that rise,
There are tears far too deep for the lakes of the eyes.

There are kisses like thistledown, fitfully sped,
There are kisses that live in the hearts of the dead.

ISOLATION

Alone! yes, evermore alone—isolate each his way,
Though hand is echoing to hand vain sophistries of clay.
Within that veiled, mystic place where bides the inmost soul,
No twain shall pass while tides shall wax, nor changing seasons roll.

Enisled, apart our pilgrimage, despite the arms that twine.
Despite the fusing kiss that wields the magic charm of wine.
Despite the interplay of sigh, the surge of sympathy.
We tread in solitude remote, the trail of destiny!

WHERE?

I called you through the silent night
 Across the brooding deep,
I sought you in the shadowland
 From out the world—asleep;

No answer echoed to my call,
 And now my way I thread
About the lowly mounds that rise
 Among the silent dead.

Though voiceless, you will hear my call,
 Your soul will heed my cry.
Will rise, and mock the prison where
 Your bones recumbent lie.

Tired

I'm tired, days and nights to me
Drag on in slow monotony,
With not a single star in sight
To lend a gleam of cheering light.

I'm tired, there are none to care
That I am drifting to despair:
O shadows! take me to your breast
For I am tired—I would rest.

Smothered Fires

A woman with a burning flame
    Deep covered through the years
With ashes. Ah! she hid it deep,
    And smothered it with tears.

Sometimes a baleful light would rise
    From out the dusky bed,
And then the woman hushed it quick
    To slumber on, as dead.

At last the weary war was done
    The tapers were alight,
And with a sigh of victory
    She breathed a soft—good-night!

The Measure

Fierce is the conflict—the battle of eyes,
Sure and unerring, the wordless replies,
Challenges flash from their ambushing caves
Men, by their glances, are masters or slaves.

Inevitably

There's nothing in the world that clings
As does a memory that stings;
While happy hours fade and pass,
Like shadows in a looking-glass.

Modulations

The petals of the faded rose
    Commingle silently,
One with the atoms of the dust,
    One with the chaliced sea.

The essence of my fleeting youth
    Caught in the web of time,
Exhales within the springing flowers
    Or breathes in love sublime.

Memory

Love's roses I gathered, all dewy, in May,
My heart holds the breath of their attar today;
And now, while the blasts of the winter winds ring,
I hear not the tempest, I'm dreaming of Spring.

Rhythm

Oh, my fancy teems with a world of dreams,—
    They revolve in a glittering fire,
How they twirl and go with the tunes that flow
    On the breath of my soul-strung lyre.

GILEAD

Walk within thy own heart's temple, child, and rest,
What you seek abides forever in thy breast.
Closer than thy folded arm
Is the soul-renewing-balm,
Walk within thy own heart's temple, child, and rest.

Foredoom

Her life was dwarfed, and wed to blight,
Her very days were shades of night,
Her every dream was born entombed.
Her soul, a bud,—that never bloomed.

Whene'er I Lift My Eyes to Bliss

Whene'er I lift my eyes to bliss,
   I stagger blind with pain,
Afar into the folding night
   The silence, and the rain.

Whene'er I feel the urge of Spring,
   A throbbing, unknown woe
Enfolds me; I am desolate
   When love is calling low.

Despair

The curtains of twilight are drawn in the west
    And vespers are sweet on the air,
While I, through my leafless, ungarlanded way
    But pause at the gates of despair.

Good-bye to the hopes that were never fulfilled,
    Good-bye to the fond dreams that failed.
Good-bye to my dead that has never been born.
    Good-bye to love's ship that ne'er sailed.

When I Am Dead

When I am dead, withhold, I pray, your blooming legacy;
Beneath the willows did I bide, and they should cover me;
I longed for light and fragrance, and I sought them far and near,
O, it would grieve me utterly, to find them on my bier!

Supreme

The fairest lips are those we kiss,
With greatest ecstasy and bliss;
The brightest eyes, are those that shine,
Unchangingly through changing time;
The greatest love is that we know.
When life is just an afterglow.

In Quest

With the first blush of morning, my soul is awing,
Away o'er the phantom lands free, wandering,
I seek thee in hamlet, in woodland, and hall.
Till night-shades, enfolding my tired heart, fall.

Yet ever and alway, like the thrush in a tree.
My heart lifts its preluding love-song to thee;
I call through the days, through the long weary years.
And slumber at night-fall, refreshed by my tears.

RECOMPENSE

Roses after rain,
Pleasure after pain,
Happiness will soothe the sigh,
Smiles await the tear-dimmed eye
Bloom will follow blight,
Daylight trails the night,
Life is sweeter
Love is deeper
In the heart's twilight!

POETRY

Behold! the living thrilling lines
That course the blood like madd'ning wines,
And leap with scintillating spray
Across the guards of ecstasy.
The flame that lights the lurid spell
Springs from the soul's artesian well,
Its fairy filament of art
Entwines the fragments of a heart.

What Need Have I for Memory?

What need have I for memory,
    When not a single flower
Has bloomed within life's desert
    For me, one little hour.

What need have I for memory
    Whose burning eyes have met
The corse of unborn happiness
    Winding the trail regret?

A Fantasy

I breathe the lyric of my love
    Across the twilit way,
The gentle echoes bear it on
    Beyond the edge of day:

All vibrant is the melody
    The silences repeat,
My song is but my longing heart
    Pulsated with its beat.

It winds amid the dusky ways
    Where far mysteries shine,
To find amid God's trackless space,
    One answering song to mine.

SOUVENIR

A little hour of sunshine,
    A little while of joy,
We winnow in our harvesting
    From all the world's alloy.

None, none, are so benighted,
    Who journey up life's hill.
But have some treasured memory,
    Which lives all vibrant still.

Illusions

Who hath not built his castles in the free and open air?
Who hath not dreamed his rosy dreams, more fair than all the fair?
Who hath not seen his castles fall, all scattered to the ground?
Who bears his dream unshattered, from the dream-land where
     they're found?

Transpositions

Smiles do not always echo cheer,
    Nor tear-drops measure grief,
For sorrow seeks a gilded mask,
    And joy in tears, relief.

THE WILLOW

When life is young, without a care,
　　Alone we walk, and free:
The world, a splendid merry round
　　Of rhythmic melody.

Before the end, grim sorrow calls
　　Into each mortal ear,
When friendship fades to memories.
　　And love lies in its bier.

Then, then it is that sympathy
　　Is holden close and dear;
Ah, then life's consolation comes
　　Commingled with a tear.

DEVASTATION

O love, you have shorn me, and rifled my heart,
You have torn down the shrine from the innermost part.
And through it now rushes a grief, sadly-wild,
That breaks as the plaint of a sorrowing child.

SPRINGTIDE

All deep there stirs the throb of Spring,
Its vital pulse I'm answering,
Swift to its dominant I merge,
One with its undulating surge;
My heart awakes to virile tone
And breaks—unanswered, and alone.

Gloamtide

The shades of the gloaming around me are stealing,
　　The lure of the dusk through the silences call,
While blossoming incense comes mutely appealing.
　　And choiring wood-voices, vespering, fall.
Immersed in the deep of my dim sylvan-bower.
　　Upborne on the breast of its emerald tide,
I drift with the gleam of the vanishing hour
　　Afar—where my uttermost longings abide.

Pendulum

I have swung to the uttermost reaches of pain,
'Mid the echo of sighs, and a deluge of rain,
But ah! I rebound to the limits of bliss.
On the rapturous swing of an infinite kiss.

DELUGE

A whisper at twilight, a sigh through the night,
A strain of soft music, a perfume so light,
Will sweep as a feather the bulwark of years,
To surges of rapture, or rivers of tears.

RETROSPECT

Love's kisses spurned so long ago,
Dead as the years, that o'er them flow;
And now, my gilded treasuries
Would I might give—for memories.

GLAMOUR

O come while youth's bright rosy veil
    Beguiles your eyes and mine,
Let's tread the asphodel of bliss,
    And drink life's magic wine:
Soon time will rend the gossamer,
    To wisdom's cruelty,
While we are blind, my love, be kind,
    For soon, too soon, we see!

The Return

Again we meet—a flashing glance,
And then, to scabbard, goes the lance,
While thoughts troop on in cavalcade
Adown the wide aisles time has made.

Back in the glow of yesterday,
With tender troth you rode away.
The sheen of rainbows in our eyes,
That swept the rim of other skies.

And now a writhing worm am I,
Beneath a doomed love's lensing eye,
Let me but stagger, far from sight.
To hide my anguish, in the night.

Love's Tendril

Sweeter far than lyric rune
Is my baby's cooing tune;
Brighter than the butterflies
Are the gleams within her eyes;
Firmer than an iron band
Serves the zephyr of her hand;
Deeper than the ocean's roll
Sounds her heart-beat in my soul.

My Little Dreams

I'm folding up my little dreams
    Within my heart tonight,
And praying I may soon forget
    The torture of their sight.

For time's deft fingers scroll my brow
    With fell relentless art—
I'm folding up my little dreams
    Tonight, within my heart.

A Note About the Author

Georgia Douglas Johnson (1880–1966) was an African American poet and playwright. Born in Atlanta, she excelled in school from a young age, learning to read, write, and play violin. She graduated from Atlanta University's Normal School in 1896 before working briefly as a teacher Marietta, Georgia. In 1902, having decided to become a professional musician, she enrolled at Oberlin Conservatory of Music, where she studied music theory and learned the art of composition. She later returned to Atlanta, marrying prominent lawyer and Republican party member Henry Lincoln Johnson, with whom she had two sons. After moving to Washington, D.C. in 1910, she embarked on a literary career against her husband's wishes, submitting poems to journals around the country. She published her first collection, *The Heart of a Woman and Other Poems* (1918) to modest acclaim and continued to grow her reputation with poems in *The Crisis*, the journal of the NAACP edited by W.E.B. Du Bois. Following her husband's death in 1925, she supported herself and her sons with various jobs and maintained a staggering output of poems, plays, short stories, and newspaper columns. She also began hosting prominent figures of the Harlem Renaissance at her home, which she called the S Street Salon, providing a meeting place for such legendary artists and intellectuals as Langston Hughes, Jean Toomer, Alain Locke, and Eulalie Spence. She is recognized today as a prominent anti-lynching activist, a pioneering poet, and one of the first African American woman playwrights.

A Note from the Publisher

Spanning many genres, from non-fiction essays to literature classics to children's books and lyric poetry, Mint Edition books showcase the master works of our time in a modern new package. The text is freshly typeset, is clean and easy to read, and features a new note about the author in each volume. Many books also include exclusive new introductory material. Every book boasts a striking new cover, which makes it as appropriate for collecting as it is for gift giving. Mint Edition books are only printed when a reader orders them, so natural resources are not wasted. We're proud that our books are never manufactured in excess and exist only in the exact quantity they need to be read and enjoyed.

bookfinity™

Discover more of your favorite classics with Bookfinity™.

- Track your reading with custom book lists.
- Get great book recommendations for your personalized Reader Type.
- Add reviews for your favorite books.
- AND MUCH MORE!

Visit **bookfinity.com** and take the fun Reader Type quiz to get started.

Enjoy our classic and modern companion pairings!

Classic & Modern